The Good Life
Perceptions of the Ordinary

The Good Life

Perceptions of the Ordinary

Jasper Morrison

Lars Müller Publishers

To Milo, Yuzuka & Masamichi

I've always liked walking around with a camera, hunting for things to take pictures of. Over the years it's evolved into something of a collector's obsession. I'm not looking to compete with real photographers for a beautiful composition or the perfect moment, but rather for a simple documenting of things I notice. For that reason I don't have a fancy camera, preferring to keep a small Canon Powershot on me whenever I can, or if not then an iPhone just about does the job. Over the years these pictures have multiplied into several thousands and with the easy visibility a computer affords I have noticed certain patterns within their number. One of these groups of images is of clever solutions to everyday problems solved with modest resources. For me this instictively human activity is the root of my profession. Without this rigorous practical thinking and the logic of common sense available to all of us, a designer had better keep his pen in his pocket. The more of these situations I gathered the more I enjoyed imagining the circumstances behind their existence. I was reading George Perec's *Life: A User's Manual* at the time, which certainly played a part in me writing these imaginings to accompany the pictures. I wrote the first one for Vitra's website in February 2009 with the idea of doing a 'picture of the month' and some of them appeared at the 2012 *Common Ground* Venice Architecture Biennale directed by David Chipperfield. This book is both the first publication and the most complete collection of them so far.

Jasper Morrison

1 Log Bench

Nobody would describe this bench as good looking, yet it has a certain charm and maybe charm is more important than looks. The bench was outside a railway station restaurant in the Japanese countryside, somewhere for people to wait for a place inside. From a design point of view there's plenty to admire. It exhibits a determined conceptual rigour, as if its maker said to himself: 'I'll make this bench from a single log of wood, 1.5 metres long, without using any screws, and it will be strong enough for an elephant and heavy enough to survive a typhoon.' The structure has been planned to make the most of a few basic cuts, so the flat sides are used for the seat (for comfort) and for the base (for stability). Its character is cheerful and welcoming, the cat enjoys the shade and it seems to deserve its place between the beer crates and the folding chair.

2 Log Pots

Continuing the theme of 'useful things to do with old trees', this picture was taken in Chandigarh on what seemed to be public land, on the road which leads to Le Corbusier's Secretariat building. Indians are well known for their ingenious re-use of materials that might seem useless to the rest of us. In this case it's the startling originality of the idea which is striking. Who would have imagined, looking at a recently cut-down tree, making three flower pots from it? And if the roadside garden is public space, how was the commission of these masterpieces briefed and to whom? In a land where this level of creativity is easily matched by that of bureaucracy, we can speculate that the order was passed down through a series of officials until it reached the urban planning office, where a young planner with an interest in gardening had the idea on his way home one evening. The best ideas are usually spontaneous.

3 Chandelier

A chandelier for the street, made from PET bottles. If this was an exhibit at the Salone del Mobile in Milan I wouldn't give it a second look. But far removed from the temptations of designer dreams, in Pondicherry, it holds a very different meaning and purpose. Hanging between two houses in the middle of a narrow residential street and consisting of some wired together PET bottles with Christmas tree lights wrapped around them, with a pulley system for lowering the assemblage for festivals or repairs, it was not so much the magnificent contrast of grandeur and lack of means that kept it hanging there, but the powerful effect it must have on the nighttime atmosphere of the street in festival. Even without its electric booster it was doing a fine job for the daytime atmosphere. No doubt it must have raised some eyebrows amongst the neighbours the day it went up, but having proven itself an asset to the community it had clearly been accepted. Ultimate proof of design quality.

4 Broken Pot

I wonder if I would have taken this photo if the pot hadn't been broken. If not, does it mean that the pot looks better broken, or simply has a better effect on the atmosphere of this courtyard in Portixol, Mallorca? Was the pot broken by the roots of the plant or by frost (not very likely), or was it a man-made accident which divided it in two? Does the owner have plans to fix it or are they not bothered by the situation? The plants themselves don't seem to mind the fault line. Closer inspection reveals the pot to be a crude concrete construction with poorly applied sea shells, edged with broken terracotta fragments and small stones, altogether surprisingly effective. The surface of the neighbouring pot, the shape of which suits the plant it contains rather well, has a similarly hand-made look, and the floor of the courtyard may well have been laid by the same craftsman, perhaps the owner himself?

5 Box Shop

Why go to the trouble of buying an expensive shop display system when
you can make one yourself? And in this case you don't have to stack the products
on the shelf or even remove them from their boxes. I suppose a certain skill is
required to avoid slicing through the merchandise while cutting the window in the
cardboard box, but it only needs doing once. The question is, is the shop keeper
lazy, or tricky, or both? Has he calulated that this device will help people to imagine
he's cheaper than anyone else, or is he so bored by the tiny profit each sale
brings that he's decided to visualise his frustration? Or is it his way of personalising
what might otherwise be a rather ordinary local shop? Has he discovered that
a help-yourself system like this one actually improves sales? Maybe the framing
around each box of products does make them seem more special than the
ones on the shelves below. Does it help us to know that the shop is in Barcelona,
in a not very rich part of town?

6 Bus Stop

We are in Pondicherry this month, more precisely Auroville, the new world city
that remains a village, to consider what may be a bus stop, or simply a shady
place to rest the feet. It stands in a clearing not far from the road, a little too far for
a bus shelter, you might think. It's an assembly of cylindrical concrete castings,
which together form a satisfying whole with combined functions. The roof is wide
enough to provide a bit of shade and shelter from the rain. A supporting column
runs from the ground up, passing through two conic cylinders that form a circular
bench with an angled back rest. I wonder what a structural engineer would say
about the connection of the roof to the supporting column, but otherwise I admire
its sculptural quality and the generosity of the idea. There was no one near it
when I stopped to take the picture, but one can imagine, besides its conceptual
elegance, an uneasy functional aspect. No problem if you're the first to arrive,
you take your seat wherever you like. But for the second there's a difficult choice
to be made: too close and the first will feel you're crowding him, and too far round,
he'll think you're ignoring him. Wherever you sit, it will be difficult to have any
conversation without some physical contortions. But maybe there's a completely
different reason for this shaded roto-bench to be here.

7 Queens

We can speculate that this industrial building standing on the corner of 10th Street and 33rd Road in Queens, New York, was originally commissioned by a small metalworking company, doing well enough to be able to afford building its own workshop. It has a purposeful appearance, lots of walls to store materials or place machinery against, lots of windows to provide the right working conditions for detailed machining operations, a very tall roller-shutter door for backing a truck in and removing large constructions. The single metal door near the corner serving as the entrance has an unusual modesty about it, suggesting the owner's briefing to the architect was a practical one, with no room for unnecessary elaboration. Why should the architecture of this buiding seem so appealing to us now? Could it be the ommission of signature, the lack of creative icing on the cake? Checking Google Maps I just discovered that the building is listed as occupied by a Fuller & Sadao Inc. – you guessed it? Buckminster Fuller and Shoji Sadao! Quite an unlikely building for architects who proposed covering Manhattan with a giant space dome, but maybe they also appreciated the no-nonsense beauty of the place, or perhaps it's just their warehouse.

8 Vase Shop

A Paris backstreet in the 3rd arrondissement, a part of town the Chinese have made their own. There are some strange shops in the area but none more intriguing than the vase shop. You wouldn't think it was a great business plan to open a shop selling only vases, and yet, perhaps it was a smart move; after all, it's still here. Let's imagine that you're Chinese and you've just moved to Paris, arriving with several suitcases stuffed with everything you think you'll need and a few reminders of home. Probably you didn't pack a vase, even though they hold an important role in the home. They are heavy and they tend to get broken, so suitcases are not the ideal place for them. No problem, the first person you ask directs you to the vase shop where you find a plentiful selection. Isn't this how shops began? Have we lost something in our compulsion for convenience? There's something heartwarming in the thought of leaving your house with the words 'I'm just popping out to the vase shop.' It's not just the very human concept of supply and demand. The advantage of the specialist provider is their ability to offer greater choice, a greater range of qualities, and professional knowledge. No doubt one day soon the vase shop will be replaced by an online service with 24-hour delivery and an even bigger choice, but the human element will be missing and you won't have quite the same relationship with the vase.

9 Melon Pack

There are some images which cannot easily be explained and this is one of them!
The facts are the following: 1. The pink, pressed cardboard-pulp packaging
was originally used for transporting melons. 2. The blue structure is a *Corse-Matin*
newspaper rack. 3. They were noticed together outside a village shop in Corsica.
4. We cannot be sure who placed the melon packaging on the newspaper
rack, or why. 5. The resulting composition is a satisfying one.

10 Museum Display

Would any western architect or designer have come up with a more beautiful or appropriate setting for the stone carvings found at the ancient and ruined city of Anuradhapura, one-time capital of Sri Lanka? The sculptures, dating from 4th century BC to 11th century AD, are set on plinths of un-mortared terracotta bricks (for the flexibility of exhibits on display?) with dividing walls of a similar brickwork, sloppily but appealingly mortared. The museum is set in an ex-British colonial mansion, and this space would probably have been the servants' quarters. The floor is now of cast concrete and the walls are white-washed. There is no lighting other than the daylight that makes it through a series of arched openings in the façade, and this soft illumination is all the sculptures need to reveal their shapes. Thinking of the fortunes spent recently on some of Europe's grand projects, one wonders if such fancy dressing does anything for the salad. How do some architects justify such enormous budgets for their projects?

11 Garden Shelves

Imagine the architect of your new house arriving one day with proposals for
the garden and, with a level voice, mentioning that the main architectural feature of
the layout will be a concrete shelving system. You do your best not to laugh out
loud and remind him that you already have plenty of shelves inside. Listen, he says,
these shelves are not for books, they are plant shelves and, being positioned as
they are on the plan, will lend your summer lunches a little privacy from the passing
neighbours. 'Ah ha! Not so stupid!' you reply, and fifty years later they are still
doing their job – almost. Despite the originality of the idea, the architect forgot that
plants on shelves need flowerpots and due to the tight spacing between them
only the top shelf would hold a reasonable sized plant. The best made plans are
full of holes!

12 Chinese Tables

A pair of identical twin tables placed side by side in an art gallery in Shanghai provides a surface for the visitors book, price list and other information on the exhibition. It seems unlikely they were made with the intention of being arranged in this way but a number of good features emerge from the partnership. First, the overall proportion is improved as it impersonates a single piece of furniture. Then we do a double take and notice that it has a certain symmetry, unusual for a console. The central leg is doubled and the lower shelf divided in two, while the front panelling is repeated twice. Was it a chance arrangement of available material, or a common device well known to the Chinese?

13 Japanese Plumbing

Is there a profession of artist plumbers? Maybe only in Japan. Think of all the wash basins you have ever seen and ask yourself if the plumbing was ever done as beautifully as this? The u-bend is a requirement of every installation, providing an air block between the basin and the drainage system below ground. Usually it's a separate unit that hangs from the underside of the water outlet with a connection to the pipework at the back, which allows the pipe to disappear into the wall horizontally. That might be preferable for cleaning the floor, but has there ever been a more poetic expression of the function than this one, which lets you know exactly where the water is going? Since writing this somone let me know that this is a standard solution in Japan.

14 Japanese Fisherman

What we have here is a museum display model of a Japanese fisherman looking for octopus and other underwater delicacies. The boat is fixed to a milky plastic sheet and provides us with a view of the fisherman from the shore, using a wooden box with a glass window at the bottom of it to get a better view of the sea bed, where he hopes to spear something tasty. Reflected in a mirror above the boat we have a sea gull's view of the boat with its equipment and of the fisherman, who we learn is kneeling on the boat's flat wooden boards with his head in a leather hood. Not a lot of extra information is gathered by the reflection and yet it draws us in and gives our imagination a richer image of the scene; we can be both the observer on land and the sea gull at the same time. A simple device that doubles the effect of the model maker's effort in setting the scene.

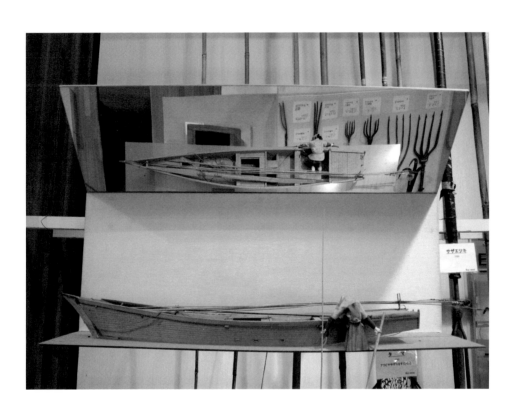

15 Octopus Pot

At first glance, in the context of a display of octopus pots, this appears to be a professional model, machine-made for the job. The flat base would sit well on the sandy depths where an octopus might need to find a hole to hide in. The rounded roof profile makes it easier to pull to the surface to check for a catch. The holes in the sides help to let all the air out on its way back down. The sliding door at the front could be quickly put in place to contain a catch. Altogether a superior upgrade on the the usual pot-shaped lobster trap. But on closer inspection it seems to be even more clever, an adaptation of a rain-water pipe. You'll notice the traces of cement at the back where the other open end has been filled, though we may assume that the slotted door closure is an option of the original manufactured pipe system and perhaps the holes too are part of the drainage equation. Whatever the truth behind the trap's origin, we can imagine that it has seen some action in the several thousand-year-old habit man has devoted to living well without much money.

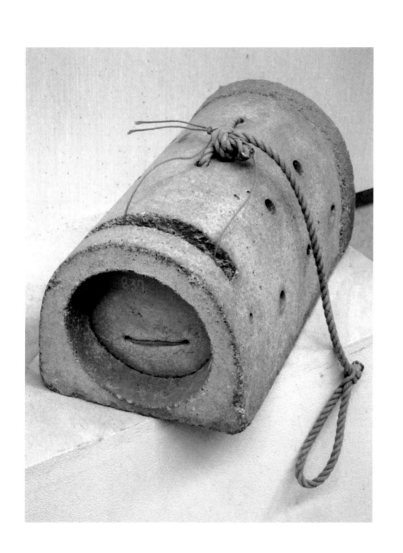

16 Paris Junkshop Window

I passed this shop window in Paris on my way for a medical check-up and raised an eyebrow at the unlikely combination of articles. I was anxious about the test that would be performed. All went well and on my way back in high spirits I stopped for a better look. It seems to me that if you wanted to make a movie out of George Perec's *Life: A User's Manual,* this would be a great way to open it. I won't go into why everyone should read this book as many times as possible, but they should. Like this junk shop window, it's a work of great optimism in the man-made world. Here we have such a cheerful composition of seemingly disconnected objects that we can't help imagining, as Perec did, the lives behind them and how they may have knowingly or unknowingly overlapped. We might also ask ourselves who created the arrangement and if they did it with calculated skill or random intuition. Either way it seemed to me a work of great beauty and faith in humanity, as convincing as anything you might find in a gallery.

17 Hook

Take a hook, any hook, and you have an interesting subject. Hooks have two basic issues to resolve, how to hang whatever they're supposed to and how to hold themselves in a position to do the hanging. In the case of this hook there are other issues. It's made to hang a pot or a kettle over a fire in the middle of a room. We don't know for sure, but we may guess that the hookmaker semi-industrialised the making of this model, or at least developed a skill to turn them out in numbers, because its construction and function show signs of highly sophisticated hookness. Taking a long, thin piece of black steel tapered towards its ends, our hookmaker has bent the two ends towards each other in a plane perpendicular to the flatness of the material, probably over some sort of former, to create an elegant hoop above the join. The hooking end comes out of the remaining joined length of the two ends. Coming back to the other issues this hook is faced with, one of them is that it has to hang over the fire by means of a chain fixed to a beam above, with a slender rod attached to the end of it. The neatness of this hook's construction is that the hoop provides the ideal means to fix the hook to the rod, with the significant added bonus of allowing the hook to rotate so that it can face the approach of the cook in any household. The cleverness of this system is only partly revealed here, so the story will be continued with a second photo.

18 Hook Part 2

Continuing the story of the hook over the fire, if we follow the rod up we find that it passes through a bracket and then enters a tube. The bracket hangs from the tube on a chain, allowing the cook to adjust the height of the hook over a fire by taking the weight off the hook and rod assembly, and thus freeing it from the bracket's grip so the rod can be slid up or down through the tube. It's tricky to describe the action in words but it's a very natural one which, with a little practice (remembering not to try it with a cast iron pot hanging from the hook!), would be almost as easy as turning the gas up or down on a modern cooker. We can imagine the superiority of this system over cruder chain and hook assemblies and the commercial advantage it gained its maker, and then realise that the design process has been around since the first bowl was formed in clay. Competition for the oldest profession?

19 Porto Garage Display

I snapped this display at a car park in Porto with my iPhone, it was either
that or leave it behind. How to explain this masterful display of plastic oil canisters,
car batteries, emergency triangles, number plates and spare hub caps? We first
assumed we'd come across an installation, part of an art project in town perhaps?
But we realised gradually that this was an innocent arrangement of things for
sale on the ramp of an underground car park. I can hear the voice of the car park's
owner discussing the idea with his manager in their neon-lit office. How are our
customers to know they can get a new battery from us if they're piled up behind
your desk? Couldn't we have a display of the things we sell? And the manager
instructing the mechanic to find somewhere to put some shelves up. Nothing special
so far, but look at the arrangement. The shelves themselves appear oddly supported
at their centres until you realise they must be two shelves joined in the middle.
The symmetry of the display starts well until, reaching the bottom shelf, car batteries
being heavy and difficult to carry up a ladder, our self-taught display artist simply
adds them to the bottom shelf nearest to his arrival, shifting out alternating oil
canisters to make space for them. So far so good, but to the mechanic's displeasure
the manager pins up a no-smoking sign and a couple of others right in the middle
of his masterpiece!

20 Porto Wheel Shop

A fine display of wheels, some of them recogniseable as standard types easily found anywhere while others have a rarer aspect. This shop in the centre of Porto would be the place to go for a replacement for your old wheelbarrow tyre or the wheel itself. Some of them look a bit more sporty, but overall the mood is an agricultural one. Easy to imagine an elderly port winemaker coming into town to pick up a new wheel for the small cart he uses to move barrels around the bodega, and he's probably known this shop all his life. Fortunately, rents in Porto are low enough to allow it to continue serving its customers, whilst elsewhere the death of the hardware shop is all but conclusive. It's a sad and unhelpful fact that the online shopping experience is so much poorer than the real thing. The physical nature of wheels demands a physical presence – the shopkeeper, the wheel and the customer should all be there for the exchange! Can anyone deny the world being a richer place with window displays like this one?

21 Army Tent

Though under armed escort, I couldn't resist shooting this arrangement on
the roof of Le Corbusier's Secretariat building in Chandigarh while my guide was
distracted. Architects are not well-known for enjoying interventions of the kind
that alter the sense of space, dignity or purpose of their buildings, but I have
a feeling Le Corbusier might have liked this one. His love and the inspiration
he drew from all things utilitarian would probably have overcome the slap in the
face that this illegal tent pitching deals out to an otherwise serious edifice.
And who cares if he would have liked it or not. Anyone with a sense of humour
and an awareness of the Indian peoples' charming and sometimes crackpot
resourcefulness will appreciate this further example of their spontaneous problem
solving. The guards need a place to rest and keep warm at night and as every
other room in the building is already taken by the bureaucrats, being army
people and enjoying the star-filled atmosphere of the camp sky, they do what
army people do everywhere else and pitch a tent.

22 Buddha

What draws the eye to this scene outside the Pondicherry Archeaolgical Museum? A headless buddha sits on a patch of grass advertsing himself with a blue sign, while behind him one of the museum's staff or a visiting professor of archeology has parked his or her bicycle next to a dramatically leaning tree. There is what looks to be a steel mailbox attached to the bicycle rack as an improvised delivery box or briefcase holder. Various potted plants make up the left side background. I'm not sure what the green cone in the foreground is, perhaps it's a light. There isn't really any further explanation coming to mind, except that sometimes a combination of absent-minded human arrangements can provide as much (or more) beauty and richness of atmosphere than one which intentionally sets out to be beautiful from the start.

23 Concrete Chair

Now who would make a chair that weighed several hundred kilograms? Generally speaking it's not advisable. There's the transport to be considered and then, when you've got it home, the lack of mobility of the item is a disadvantage. There's one near Venice on the island of Torchello made several hundred years ago and there are other seats weighing in at similar levels, but these were made for kings and queens in an attempt to emphasise the permanence of their power. I am guessing that the owner of this one is far from powerful and it was almost certainly not custom made as a chair at all. Sitting in an enclosure near the beach to the north of Pondycherry with its back leaning unneccessarily against a feeble shack, it looked like a nice place to sit. But who dragged it here and went to the trouble of building a foundation for it to have a better sitting height? Why did they think the back needed to be supported, did they think it would tip over!? And what was it originally made as? I wasn't able to find anyone to ask and I am lost for any explanation, so it remains a mystery of the world of chairs.

24 Japanese Garden

We are used to seeing images of perfect Japanese gardens, clipped and preened like poodles, though never kitsch. We marvel at the conceit of rocks and trees tamed and trained like circus animals, putting on a show to outperform the real thing. Yet in these idyllic compositions there's a 'look but don't touch' atmosphere, which ultimately prevents most of them from succeeding. When I came across this scene at a handmade paper workshop in Gifu it seemed to be all about the incongruity of the light blue plastic crate in a natural setting, but looking at it again it's the crate which makes the setting more natural. It's a human instinct to make use of convenient situations, and a flat topped rock is just the place to set down a plastic crate because it's heavy or just to get it out of the way. Treating the rock like a real rock instead of a precious element of the composition allows us to perceive everything, if not as a natural scene then at least as a scene made more natural by evidence of the life going on around it.

25 Wooden Spoons

Back to Porto again, where they not only sell wooden spoons in all sizes
but have a small street of shops which offer them, and what a window display!
I sometimes feel while walking around this town that I am in a dream where
all the stupid values that are attached to useless things have been reversed, only
useful things are in demand, and where a nail can still be bought from a wooden
box. A world free of blister-packed goods from distibuters of cheaply made junk
from far away places, where the small scale manufacture of something useful
and charming still has a place. How can it be that corporate tentacles have not
yet strangled this beautiful place? It's tempting to imagine Porto might survive,
like an old paperback copy of George Perec's short writings, largely ignored but
full of interest and quality.

26 Lingerie Shop

I have to admit I found this lingerie shop display in a Barcelona alley rather exciting. Something to do with the twin volumes and the tensioned straps, I think, though it would take a good psychologist to unravel the threads of erotic appeal from the purely sculptural. It reminds me of a scene from a Fellini film in which Marcello Mastroiani dreams he's the only man left in a world full of women. It starts out well for him but ends badly. The shop has to be one of the least visible windows in town and I only came across it attempting a short cut to a restaurant. I suppose the owner, aware of the lack of passing trade, must have taken the decision to go for maximum visual impact in the hope of being noticed. It certainly worked with me. Looking closer, we see that each bra has a name and a price, Bianca 12.40, Gloria 11.90, Paloma 13.90, etc. and that behind the displayed articles catalogue pages have been attached to the supporting panels, creating the mesmerising effect of several invisible women lying on top of as many visible ones, all wearing bras. Five-star window dressing in my humble opinion.

27 'Yes We Sell' Sign

Let's imagine you're walking down a street and you pass a timber shop. Some steps later you remember that you need a piece of hardboard (a thin and cheap, honey-coloured sheet material with one side smooth, which the British love to use for quick repairs). There's a dangerous hole on the staircase of the house you've just moved into and you need to fix it. The shop is J. Matthias on Hackney Road in East London and you are not the first person to ask him if he has hardboard and can cut you a piece to size. Yes, he does and yes, he can. He seems irritated by the question, and later over lunch with his wife it all comes out. He's sick of people asking him the same question, of course he sells hardboard and can cut it to size, that's his job, isn't it? Why not put up a sign then, so they wouldn't have to keep asking? Silenced by his wife's perfect logic, he finishes his lunch in deep thought. A couple of pieces of board fixed together from behind, painted white, and what's left of the pot of brown paint should be enough for his message. If you have ever tried painting letters with a brush you'll know how difficult it is, and though we will never know how he managed such graphic perfection, we can guess that he spent some time preparing for it. The tops and bottoms of the letters all line up, the straight strokes are mostly perfectly straight and the spacing and alignment are almost professional. The shop's no longer there, but the sign now hangs on the living room wall of a friend of mine who managed to rescue it before it closed down.

28 Brick Door and Window

Someone went to the trouble of painting this wall white while leaving the shape of a door and window unpainted. I walked past it several times before asking myself why it was done and what message it sends. The wall in question is in the entrance hall of Vitra AG's product development centre in Birsfelden, near Basel. I asked around the company and it seems there was once a door and window in these positions and that at a certain moment they were no longer needed. The frames were removed and the openings closed with matching brickwork which, without the intervention of the boss who appreciated the eccentricity of this architectural memory, would have been lost forever behind matching white paint.

29 Lifiting Gear

I don't know much about lifting heavy things but I'm guessing that if you needed to find out or get the right equipment, this shop in Tokyo would have been the place to go. I like the semi-organised display of rings, hooks and hoops, with rings and hooks organised left to right, big to small, then hoops somewhat out of order. I admire these serious things which cannot be allowed to fail, cheerful in their bright orange paint (and one in a bordeaux red), the hooks with sky blue safety catches. Against a stepped black background they present themselves like a team line-up, each group with its particular position to play in the lifting game. The shop closed down a few years ago and the neighbourhood, losing an industrial ingredient, tipped another degree towards residential. It was right next to the local park and the three-storey building it occupied was immediately replaced by a twelve-storey apartment block. The combined forces of land value and internet selling claiming another victim and impoverishing the local atmosphere.

30 Man Buying Mochi

Over how many thousands of years has this everyday ritual been played out? In this case, a man out for a walk on a Tokyo street, his head turned by a display of cakes, takes another step before pausing to examine the offering, confirms his first impulse was the right one, checks the price and makes his order. The shopkeeper wraps it up while the man waits to pay. A perfectly normal routine and yet increasingly rare. Money changes hands from one local to another for goods, in this case 'mochi' rice cakes, made in the back of the shop, the rice probably supplied by another local business. The man's salary or pension recycled and kept in the neighbourhood. Cycled on again at the butcher's or the grocer's instead of being sucked out by a supermarket or convenience store chain. A decline of the local quality of life, but not irreversable. As local shops close down under pressure from web selling, store rents should reduce, leaving opportunites for newer local models; *Super Normal* retailing.

31 Nails

Nails have to be amongst the most democratic of inventions. Cheap, readily available, easy to use, and allowing the user to improve the conditions of daily life with a few blows of the hammer. Whatever the act involving a nail – hanging a picture, repairing a cupboard, re-fixing a floor board, putting up a calendar – the equation of effort to reward is always a satisfying one. These ships' nails seen at Sheikh Faisal's Museum outside Doha are no exception and reveal the incredible potential of this humble article. With nails, a boat could be made more quickly and cheaply and with a boat more fish could be caught. More fish caught could be sold for less, leaving everyone with money for nails!

32 Hosepipe Wheel

Where there's a problem and an easy solution is discovered by someone, it's quickly adopted by others. How many wheels have been bolted to walls to provide an easy and convenient way to store a garden hose pipe? Someone must have been the first to think of it but we'll never know who. Another mystery is where the wheels come from. Let's say that you have an old and broken car which isn't worth fixing. You might not think of removing its wheels in case, one day, you take up gardening and need one to store a hosepipe. And if you did, how could the car be towed away? And when you decide you need a wheel on the side of your shed, where do you get one? You could take off a front wheel perhaps and the car could be towed away on its back wheels. But there's a simpler answer: cars have spare wheels!

33 Wild Flower Display

Has there ever been a better way invented to display wild flowers? I came across this former PET bottle in Shirakawa-go, a much visited, traditional Japanese village consisting of several giant thatched farmhouses. The bottle has had its label removed, and two small holes have been made neatly in one side, into which the funnel ends of two similar bottles have been screwed, allowing the Ikebana enthusiast to prepare two different but complimentary displays in one 'vase'. Even the stems play a part in the display.

34 Istanbul Fishing

There are many of these fishing rods clamped to the Galata Bridge in Istanbul, which suggests that there must be a lot of aquatic traffic in the waters between Europe and Asia. I noticed several rods using the same simple wooden bracket and giant elastic band combination to provide a suitable rest for the rod, allowing the fisherman to take his time preparing bait, talk to a neighbour, look across the water with arms folded and resting on the rail, or eat a sandwich. I admired the simplicity of the fixation and the double notch to keep the rod straight and, in the event of bite, to prevent it flipping into the sea until the fisherman has it safely in hand. I like to imagine the inventor, a carpenter, turning up with the first of these and one by one having to make more for his fellow fishermen.

Jasper Morrison

Born in London in 1959, Jasper Morrison works as a designer between London, Paris and Tokyo. His designs are produced in Europe, USA and Japan by leading manufacturers of furniture, lighting, electronics, shoes, wristwatches and more. He has also published a number of books including *A World Without Words, Super Normal* (co-authored with Naoto Fukasawa), *Everything but the Walls, A Book of Things,* and *The Hard Life* (Lars Müller Publishers), *A Book of Spoons* (Imschoot Uitgevers), and *Jasper Morrison au Musée* (Bernard Chauveau).

The Good Life
Perceptions of the Ordinary
Jasper Morrison

Design: Jasper Morrison with Integral Lars Müller
Text editing: Laura McLardy
Lithography: Ast & Fischer, Wabern
Printing and binding: Eberl & Koesel, Altusried-Krugzell, Germany
Paper: Condat matt Périgord, 150 g/m^2

Lars Müller Publishers
Zürich, Switzerland
www.lars-mueller-publishers.com

ISBN 978-3-03778-423-5

Distributed in North America by ARTBOOK | D.A.P.
www.artbook.com

Printed in Germany